Growing Your Lavender Garden

BOOK TWO

D1571985

Elizabeth Inman

DuBeau Press
PO Box 939
Abiquiu, NM 87510

Second Edition
Printed in the United State of America
ISBN 978-0-9977120-0-1
(paperback)

To my mother,
Bette Lee,
who taught me to love and care for my gardens

Contents

AUTHOR'S NOTE
Guidebook for Lavender Lovers

~

GROWING YOUR LAVENDER GARDEN IS a guidebook for lavender lovers and is presented in a series of three parts that follow the seasons, starting with the idea of growing lavender, continuing with caring for and preserving your lavender, and ending with making something lovely with the lavender you have grown in your garden. They are sweet and easy to follow, and they will aid you in having your own beautiful and productive lavender garden that gives joy with minimal labor. You will find all three parts useful and a must-have for practical assistance in the care of and creating with your lavender.

The information contained in this book is easy and comprehensive. You will have enough knowledge on growing lavender to start your lavender garden, maintain it, and know what to do with your lavender after harvest. We will finish off part 3 with the subject of crafting and DIY items that can come from your lavender garden and you can make in your own kitchen. They are simple recipes that are a good entrance into your imagination. Once you see what you can use your lavender for, it opens up a whole world of ideas.

Part 1 you will learn how to design your garden, choose varieties, understand the planting process, and care for your lavender.

Designing and planting your lavender garden will be the most work you will do in caring for your plants. Putting your time and effort in up front at the planning stage will save you miles of headache and disappointment in your garden in the future. I will tell you step-by-step how to have a healthy, happy lavender garden that will bring you years of joy.

Part 2 you will learn how to harvest, prune, and dry your lavender for use at a later time. You will learn about pruning and why it is important for your lavender. You will also learn how to make the most out of growing and having lavender. You will learn how to harvest and prune your plants and why this is so important for the care of your lavender. The best news is that I will show you how to make this easy and to prune each plant in under thirty seconds. You will also learn how to prepare your lavender for use and how to store it properly if you want to use it later. You do not need to use your harvest immediately. If it is properly stored, you can save it for when the time is right for you to create and work on a project with your lavender. You will learn how to prepare your lavender for making crafts or wonderfully scented DIY lavender products. Saving your lavender carefully and properly will protect it for quite some time, even years. Learn how to use fresh lavender for table bouquets and potpourris. This booklet will show you how to prepare your lavender garden for winter and what to expect when your lavender wakes up in the spring.

Part 3 will teach you the basics on how to make attractive lavender gifts and to use lavender in different ways in your home and on your body. You will learn how to make lovely scented lavender crafts harvested right from your garden. You will have enough information so you can fashion your own unique creations.

There are many ideas for making safe and effective products using lavender essential oil and raw ingredients that can be purchased at your local store or online. Part 3 will cover some crafting ideas for holidays or special gift giving, and these DIY ideas are easy and can be made right in your own home. These are ideas that are taken from concept to finished product and can be used for years to come. Enjoy the fun of making something from the lavender garden you have lovingly grown.

Designing and Growing Your Lavender Garden

⟋⟍

IF YOU WANT AN EXQUISITE garden filled with lovely lavender to adorn your space and you want something that does not require exhaustive amounts of time and labor, then lavender may be for you. There is nothing so beautiful as a spring garden coming to life with the fragrant scents of lavender that fill the air and please the soul.

Taking care of a lavender garden can be an easy and rewarding experience if you choose the right plants. What are the right plants? They are the ones that fit your space, are the right size, are the correct zone, and are the right variety to use for crafting. They will be the varieties you need for crafting, cooking, or just enjoying a lovely bundle of lavender sitting on your table. They need so little and give so much, and adding beautiful lavender to your garden can be a deeply satisfying experience. If you love to dig in the dirt and enjoy the process, you can create a beautiful garden of lavender.

I have spent my life creating and tending my gardens. My biggest garden is the Purple Adobe Lavender Farm in Abiquiu, New Mexico.

I have been growing and creating with lavender since 2004, and the farm now has over five thousand lavender plants in the ground. Lavender has taught me the truths from the myths of growing this wonderful plant, making it easier than you would think. Lavender is a resilient plant and has many healing properties, and it offers peace and beauty to its owner. It is beautiful on so many levels and is quite possibly the most-loved plant of the twenty-first century.

The Purple Adobe Lavender Farm is an agritourism destination farm where guests can come for a day or stay in our vacation-rental casita for a longer visit. We have created an educational environment for those who want to learn to grow lavender. We propagate and grow between three thousand and five thousand lavender plants each year. We sell our plants out of our Zen nursery, where you can receive instructions on how to grow and care for your new lavender plant. We have helped start farms and projects throughout New Mexico and continue to spread the word of the many benefits of growing and having lavender. We manufacture over seventy all-natural aromatherapeutic products made from our organically grown lavender that are available for purchase in our country store here on the farm. We are host to over ten thousand guests per year who come to enjoy beauty, a little peace, and the scent of lavender.

In this book, I will talk about the dos and don'ts of growing lavender and what a lavender garden needs in order to thrive with little work from you. Most gardens take hours and days of attention but not lavender. I will show you how to have a lavender garden with minimal effort. There are many ways to design lavender gardens, and you can choose one that fits your needs.

Certain varieties work well for creating garden paths or lining walkways, or you can fill your area with a sea of purple lavender. I will suggest some of the many varieties you can choose from to design your perfect lavender garden. Different varieties work better for different planting areas, and I will show you how to choose a variety that will work best for your planting. Sometimes finding lavender can be difficult, so I will suggest some resources. Whatever your choice, you can have a garden of lavender that will give you immense joy.

Choosing the right lavender for your garden will give you years of enjoyment. It can be a rewarding experience when your garden is an expression of your vision and planning. You can have a lavender garden just for the sheer beauty of having it, or you can choose to use your lavender to make special gifts or freshly cut bundles to scent your home with an intoxicating fragrance. You may want to maximize your garden with lavender choices that bloom at different times. This will extend your lavender garden's blooming time. Nonetheless, whether you choose tall or short, big or small, or early or late blooming, you can plan it and enjoy it for years.

There are some of the sweetest-scented lavenders that add a delightful hint of lavender to your culinary dish. You may want to plant a charming English garden with lavender and herbs; this is a perfect combination.

You could choose to plant your lavender garden with complementary plants, using larger varieties that make a bold statement, or you could choose a garden that says, "Just come and sit with me, and I will give you peace and beauty."

No matter which garden design you choose, having the right variety is an important decision when growing lavender. Knowing how to choose what you need will make for a happy lavender experience.

Some varieties have similarities but also can have vastly different characteristics. This book will aid you in simplifying the process. Taking time to plan will be well worth the effort. Use the blank pages in the back of the book to lay out your design or take notes of important facts you may want to remember in designing your garden. This is how the fields of the Purple Adobe Lavender Farm were done. Each field was laid out on paper, planned, and researched for performance and durability before planting. Planning ahead helped us to stay organized and could be helpful for you too.

As in anything, most of the work is done in the beginning, and knowing how your decisions make your garden what it will be tomorrow will be a rewarding experience.

Let's move forward and begin your lavender garden.

PART 1
Designing Your Garden

⤨

DECIDING TO PLAN AND PLANT a lavender garden will be one of the most rewarding experiences in your life. Designing and planting will be the most work you will do in caring for your plants. Having and caring for a lavender garden is fairly easy and can give you immense joy. Putting in your time and effort up front in the planning stage will save you miles of headache and disappointment with your garden in the future. My mother always said to me, "Anything worth doing is worth doing well." So let's dig in, and I will tell you how to have a healthy, happy lavender garden that will bring you years of joy.

When designing your lavender garden, there are a few things to consider. We will go over all these items in this chapter. There are decisions you will need to make about the following:

- spacing
- size
- shape
- variety and cultivars, and
- irrigation types

Lavender is a social plant and does not like to be planted alone. It prefers the company of other plants. Whether you choose to have a full garden of lavender or a mixture of plants, be sure to put plants in the garden that have the same watering needs. Many plants require water several times per week, but lavender is not one of them. Too much water will, without any doubt, kill your plant. Lavender is drought tolerant, but it is not xeric. A xeric plant is one that can survive on rainfall with little to no additional water. If a plant is drought tolerant, that means it will use less water than most plants and cannot survive with no extra water. It does *not* need to be watered daily or even every other day, for that matter. And once the plant is fully established, you can water once a week or even stretch watering out to ten days. Be sure to select accompanying plants that have similar growing and watering needs. I will talk about this further in the section on watering.

Spacing

Spacing your plants to the appropriate distance will allow them to get plenty of air around them and extend to their fullest reach. If your plants are too close, they will not perform well and will not reach their greatest beauty. They will become tangled and will not be able to have that traditional dome shape. If you decide to move them later, there is a good chance they will not survive. Lavender does not like to be transplanted. It is best to take the time while you are in the planning stage and draw out your garden with the correct distance between plants.

Size

Two of the most basic genera of lavenders we will be working with are the French lavender *Lavendula x intermedia* and the English lavender *Lavendula angustifolia*.

French lavenders are bigger, have longer stems, and will spread out more. They look wonderful in areas that have a large space available and demand a bold statement. They range in size from 3 to 5 feet across and can have up to 1,700 stems of lovely blooms. This varietal is quite outstanding; they have a stronger scent and are great for making lavender bundles and bouquets. Planting requirements are 3.5 to 4.5 feet on centers. That measurement is determined from the center of the lavender to the center of the neighboring plant.

English lavenders have shorter and more compact stems. They range in color from deep purple to light lavender and some pink. English lavender is quite special for smaller gardens, pathways, and herb gardens. They can be placed in areas in which space is limited and you want a more compact and controlled lavender. The size can range from 2 to 3.5 feet across, and they possess a sweeter scent that is more floral and delicate. This lavender can be used for sweeter culinary dishes and is wonderful for French bouquets. The English variety of lavender is wonderful for wedding bouquets. This is because the flowers stay truer to their color and tend to remain on the stem longer.

These choices will be important when planning your garden. You will need to know this when you go shopping for your lavender plants. Knowing how you want to use your lavender will aid you in choosing the right lavender for your garden.

With so many subspecies and varieties of lavender within the French and English cultivars, it is likely your nursery will not know the difference and not be able to advise you correctly. If this is so, knowing whether you want a larger French or a smaller English lavender will help with choosing the right plant for your garden, and this will be the most important part. You can find some lovely varieties within those two cultivars that will work well in your garden. Be sure to read the tag and look for the Latin names *Lavendula x intermedia* (French) and *Lavendula angustifolia* (English) so you will know what you are buying. Knowing the exact variety is not nearly as important as knowing whether your cultivar is French or English.

You should also check the zone to be sure it will grow in your area. This will be important when purchasing your lavender. Lavender plants brought in from other states have been grown in greenhouses and could be a different zone. They are most likely zones seven and eight, so be sure they will grow in your area. If you live in a lower zone, the plants will not survive through winter in a zone lower than a seven or eight, so check your plants before you purchase them to be sure you have the variety that will survive in your zone, or you will end up with a plant that lives as an annual because it will die over the winter.

The English lavenders are traditionally darker in color, have a sweeter floral scent, and grow more compactly in growth patterns. The French lavenders are lighter in color; have a stronger, more intense fragrance; and have longer square stems that spread out. Chances are you will not know the difference when purchasing your plant, as they all look pretty much alike at the nursery stage, so knowing your cultivars will be your biggest help.

If your nursery cannot provide you with the plants or information you need, you can find many lavender plants online at www.highcountrygardens.com, and they will ship your plants. Also, if you are near our farm, we grow and sell many plants a year, so you can purchase them on the farm from us. We do not ship plants.

With literally hundreds of varieties available, it will be difficult to get most varieties from your local nursery, but you will have fun looking for different varieties to adorn your garden. There is a lot of information to be found by searching specific plants online. The most important choice is knowing the difference and choosing between French and English.

SHAPE

The shape of your garden is limited only by your imagination. There are so many different designs. Most gardens are determined by the space that is available and how they can enhance the area of space.

If your garden design has a flat background, such as up against a house or a wall, then you could place your larger French lavender plants in the back so they do not dwarf or hide your lovely English lavender in the front areas. If you are planting in an open garden with no sides, then placing your French lavenders in the middle of the garden area would give a beautiful presentation. In a free-form garden, imagine a winding S- or C-shaped design that runs through the center of the garden filled with smaller English lavender plants to follow the organic winding direction. If your space allows, you could place a small bench in the center of the garden and have a winding path leading to the seating area, where you can sit in your lavender garden, creating a beautiful focal point for your property.

Drawing your plan on paper will help you stay organized and give you a great visual for how it will turn out. You can use the blank paper in the back of this book for your notes and for creating your design. This will help you get started with some ideas for your garden's design.

VARIETIES AND CULTIVARS

Varieties are those that you will be looking for when selecting your plants. The most standard are subcategories of English, French, and Spanish. Varieties such as Grosso, Provence, Hidcote, and Buena Vista are popular in many lavender gardens. There are so many varieties to choose from; you will enjoy searching for the different lavenders and making discoveries on your own. Search on Google for "different varieties of lavender plants," and then select "Images" from the top menu. Remember, when searching for lavender, the varietal choices that are important are "French" and "English." You will find many subspecies of these two varietals. You will never be able to find all the species in a nursery, so check online, and then you can search through www.highcountrygardens.com, and they ship. That will give you lots of lavender eye candy to peruse. Remember that size is important for your design. The two considerations for our purposes are English and French—just remember that English is smaller and French is larger. This is a simple and basic distinction that will make your selection easier.

Planting several different varieties will give your garden a longer blooming period. The English lavender are early bloomers, and French lavender will blossom later and at different times within their own species. With some varieties of English, you may get a second blooming, such as with Buena Vista, which is known for its second blooming. Thus, after the French lavender blooms, you will have yet another blooming from your Buena Vista, giving you an even longer period of blooming for your garden. If you live in zones six, seven, or eight, you will get a second bloom on almost all of your lavender. In lower zones such as four and five, you will get second blooms on some of your English lavender. If you are planting along a walkway, you probably would want all of your lavender to bloom at the same time. The varieties you choose will be specific to the area you are planting.

Companion planting can be a lovely decision to add movement and dimension to your garden. Some of my favorite companion plants for lavender are ornamental grasses. They give that movement to your garden and do not encroach on other plants. There are so many lovely varieties, and they help in extending your beautiful garden's growing season. I cannot stress enough how important it is when planning to buy your plants that you check the zone to ensure their success in your garden. There are some stunning grasses available, but they are zone specific; some may not grow in your area, so be sure what you are buying.

Here at the Purple Adobe Lavender Farm, we grow and sell several zone four varieties, and we have helped start many lavender gardens and farms in our area. Buying from a local source has its benefits because the grower usually sells from their own stock and knows what grows best in that region. Try looking online for lavender farms in your area. They usually sell plants that are specific to your zone.

Irrigation Types

Lavender needs to be watered from under the plant, so it is a good idea to put in a drip system for watering. Watering overhead can damage your plants in many ways. Water from a drip system will give you more control and uniformity when watering. It is easy to purchase a drip hose and drippers from your local hardware store that will attach to your main watering system. We use drippers that emit a half gallon per hour (giving one gallon of water per hour), and there are two drippers per plant, one on each side of the plant about five inches away from the trunk.

This watering system is not an absolute rule, but it is what we have found to be best for the plant. If this is not an option and it will not work for your system, there are irrigation systems you can attach right to your garden hose. You can use a soaker hose that can be placed permanently at the base of your plants running throughout your garden, and the end will attach to your garden hose. These can be held in place using U-pins. You can purchase these at your garden store.

Watering by hand is not advisable. Not only will it add to the labor of your garden, but when you lose interest and consistency in watering or when you go away on vacation, your plants will begin to show signs of distress and die off. Plan on a watering system that is easy for you and healthy for your plants. This decision needs to be made at the planning stage so you are ready to start your irrigation as soon as you have planted your garden.

Preparing Your Garden

Now that you have decided to plant your lavender garden, here are some important considerations for the planting. Lavender has few needs; it will be one of the easiest plants you will grow. For the success of your lavender garden, you will need basic knowledge of the following;

- sun
- soil
- watering
- where to create your garden
- elevation and location
- fertilization
- diseases and insects
- mulching
- planting checklist
- planting instructions

Sun

Sun is your first consideration. Where are you going to put your garden? Sun to flowers is like water to humans, it is essential. Lavender will not produce without the warmth and light of the sun. When you are deciding where to create your garden, here are a few important tips. Choose an area that gets full sun. The more sun you have, the more flowers the plant will produce and the healthier your lavender will be. Lavender needs a minimum of six hours of sun a day but will be happier with more. Planting in a southern- or western-facing exposure is preferable because it offers the most hours of sun in a day.

If you live in an area that freezes in the winter, these placements will help your plant go through the winter months with a little extra warmth. It actually will raise the zone and microclimate the area, making it a bit warmer.

Here are a few exceptions: if you live in an extremely hot area—I mean Arizona, Nevada, or Oklahoma type of hot—then planting on an eastern exposure would be a better choice. The sun and heat are so intense in these regions that it actually will cause distress to the plant, and it may not bloom at all. If you consistently have heat over one hundred degrees during your summer months, it would be preferable to plant on an easterly facing exposure so your lavender can make it through scorching days.

Soil
Surprisingly, the soil is the least important of all your decisions. Lavender can thrive in the poorest of soils. There are only a couple of rules when it comes to soil: it must drain well, and it must contain no clay. If you plant in clay soil, it is not a matter of if but when your lavender will succumb to death. Lavender is not too picky about the soil and will grow in rocky, sandy, and nonfertilized soils, but it is critical that the soil drains well. Clay soil does not drain well, so it is best to stay away from planting in such areas, as they become sticky and allow no air to the roots, a certain death for lavender.

A very easy way to determine whether your soil drains well is to choose an area in which you want to plant. Dig a hole about a foot deep, and fill it with water. Watch to see how long it takes to drain, and then fill it again. If it drains in less than half an hour, you are fine. If it takes more than half an hour, then it is a pretty good indicator of where *not* to plant your lavender. You can amend the soil with a soil amender, but it is best to plant somewhere else. If there is nowhere else to plant, you will need to amend the soil. Take out the old soil two feet down and two feet wide, and replace it with a good composted soil. Place some rocks in the bottom of the hole to create a small French drain.

The soil should be light and loose when planting, so plan to open up your soil by digging your holes and loosening the soil surrounding the area in which your plant will be placed. You can do this with your hands—just break up the soil so it has no hard clumps in it. Dig the hole twice the size of the pot; for example, if your pot is six inches in diameter, dig the hole to twelve inches. When you plant, you can then add loose composted soil mixed with the soil you broke up around the root base. Light and airy soil will encourage the roots to stretch out and grow in their new home.

Lavender is an alkaline-loving plant, so a soil that is above seven on the pH scale is a plus. You can choose to have your soil tested by checking with your local agricultural center. They will advise you where to have your soil sent for testing. For an ornamental garden, it really is not critical or even necessary. But if you are planning a large planting or a commercial installation, it would be reasonable to take this extra step.

Remember that if you give lavender what it needs up front and do not sidestep these few rules, you will have years of enjoyment from your lavender plants. Lavender has few requirements to grow and be successful, and if you tend to these requirements, you will have healthy, happy lavender.

WATERING

The motto for lavender is that less is more. It is a drought-tolerant plant, so less water is more beneficial. Good drainage is a necessity, as it does not like its feet kept wet. It wants to be drenched and then drained. This is one of the most important requirements in growing lavender.

Lavender does not like its roots kept wet; it likes the drenched-and-then-drained process. This means that you should water it well and then allow it to drain and dry out to almost dry. Watering too often will smother and rot the roots. That's why planting with like-kind plants (plants that have the same watering requirements) is a good idea. The lavender will not do well otherwise. Even if you put your lavender on a separate watering zone from your neighboring plants, the soil will hold too much water and be too wet; the plants will do poorly or even die.

Placement of your dripper is important. Many people think it is good to place the dripper right at the trunk of a plant, but this is *not* the case with lavender. Place your dripper about four to six inches away from the trunk. Too much water at the trunk will rot the trunk and leave the soil too wet, which will stress the plant, so be sure to water around the plant and not directly at the trunk. Also, be sure *not* to create wells at the base of your plant. This sounds like a good idea, but it will allow too much water to accumulate at the base. By placing your dripper away from the trunk, it will keep it from drowning the plant and rotting the trunk. This will encourage the roots to stretch out, offering you a healthier plant.

Acclimating your plant to a new environment can be a bit of a dance. Too much water or too little water can hinder the plant in adjusting to its new home and can lead to its demise.

Putting water on every day is too much. If your plant is a bit cooler because it does not get full sun and the soil stays damp or even wet, then watering every day will for sure kill your plant because the soil will stay wetter. Water thoroughly when you first plant, and then check the soil daily or at least every other day. It is best to put your fingers down into the soil around the plant to see exactly what is happening. If the soil is drying out, then it is okay to water. If your soil is still too wet, leave it alone and check it the next day. Because your lavender plant is new, it will require more water until it shows signs of being at home in its new environment. So you may be watering every other day, every third day, or even every fourth day, just not every day. By using this method, you will get to know your soil well and become an expert on how to water your lavender. Lavender is a Mediterranean plant and prefers a drier climate. Don't be worried if the soil begins to dry out; that is what you want it to do. Using the drench-and-drain method is a good rule of thumb for watering.

Where to Create Your Garden

The choices are endless for where lavender can grow. If you follow the above guidelines on sun and soil, you can plant almost anywhere. You can plant a garden edging a path to your home or plant a garden under your window so the scent will drift in during the blooming season. Lavender does wonderfully in a courtyard or in a tiered garden.

Encircle your house with lavender, and add a little color, such as yellow, to complement the lavender hue.

If you have a botanical garden in your area, that is a great place to get ideas for your design, and they are quite helpful with the planting process. Look into some of the garden books at your local nursery or newsstand to get ideas for your design. You do not need to follow them exactly, but they are good for inspiration to get started designing your garden. Remember three things when you are planning your garden: (1) water requirements must be the same as neighboring plants, and the soil must have good drainage, (2) soil requirements should be similar, and (3) pay attention to plant spacing needs.

Most of your work is done in the planning stages. Choose plants to accompany your lavender that do not require a lot of maintenance. Lavender needs little attention throughout the year; keep your garden simple so you are not laboring over it all year. If you choose to have lavender with some ornamental grasses, which is one of my favorite garden complements, you will discover there is little maintenance in caring for your gorgeous lavender garden. Lavender that is planted along with ornamental grasses gives movement to your garden and can be quite lovely.

ELEVATION AND LOCATION

Lavender can grow almost anywhere, with some exceptions. Lavender does not thrive above eight thousand feet; it is too cold. Quite possibly if your lavender is planted in a southern exposure with other elements around it, such as a courtyard or a solid fence, or if it is against the house, the plant will get extra protection. This will microclimate the area, and it will be able to pull heat from the house during cold winter months. If you live at eight thousand feet and simply *must* have lavender, you can plant against the south-facing wall (maybe in a courtyard) where the plant will be protected from cold wind. If you also have less than two feet of snow in the winter, you might be the miracle green thumb who can pull it off. If you are determined, knowing you are going against the odds, then I think you could do it, but I wouldn't try planting a field. You are headed for heartache.

Planting under shade trees looks beautiful, but lavender does not like that placement, as the soil is too acidic, and the roots will compete for space and moisture. Do not plant in or around any kind of pine tree or forested trees; the needles and the soils are not beneficial for lavender. They look amazing within a rose garden, but the two plants have completely different sets of needs and do not mix well. If you choose to try to plant roses and lavender together, each must be on its own watering zone, and it is best to keep the lavender on the perimeter and not too close to the roses. English lavender would be a better choice if you want to chance this design, as it better handles a wetter environment and could possibly survive within a rose garden.

It is good to remember that lavender is a Mediterranean plant that loves an arid climate. They thrive in dry areas. Plants that have similar habits will make for a more successful garden.

FERTILIZATION

The great news is; lavender needs no fertilization and will bloom beautifully year after year without being fertilized. This makes lavender a very attractive choice in the garden because it has few, if any, requirements for additives. It is beautiful and has so many physical, emotional, and spiritual benefits, making it one of the most loved and beneficial plants to have in your garden.

When you plant your lavender, you can add a handful of organic fertilizer. This is to encourage the roots to reach out and acclimate to the soil. Here on the lavender farm, we add one handful of Yum Yum Mix—an organic fertilizer—while planting. The hole is mixed with one half soil and one-half composted horse manure, and then we mix in the Yum Yum. This gives the plant a good start. You can use this mixture, or you can use composted soil instead of the horse manure. This is available for purchase at your local nursery. Lavender will grow and thrive in rocky, sandy, or nutrient-poor soil without the addition of fertilizer.

If your plant shows signs of distress, it is not because it needs fertilizer or water. There is something else happening that is causing this distress. Check your soil to see whether it is too wet; don't add water unless it is on the dry side. Reference the "Dos and Don'ts of Growing Lavender" checklist to see where you may have gone off track. Remember, lavender has few requirements to thrive and be a gorgeous addition to your garden. If you follow the guidelines in this book, you can have that gorgeous lavender garden you have always wanted.

DISEASES AND INSECTS

Here's more good news: lavender has only a few possibilities for diseases and even fewer for insects. It is one of the easiest plants to grow because it has so few needs. Lavender has a bitter taste, so bugs and animals just don't bother, especially if there is something tastier in the garden. Domestic pets may want to snuggle in them, but they won't eat the plant. It is more likely the surrounding plants will develop a disease or an animal vulnerability than your lavender will. This is a good reason to select accompanying plants to be of a similar kind or to just plant lavender in the garden. Choose plants that have the same watering, soil, and sun needs and that have little to no disease and pest vulnerability. By doing this, you will keep a pleasing, enjoyable, and almost labor-free garden.

If you live in a rural area, you will no doubt have animals in the wild coming for a visit. They will most likely bypass the bitter-tasting lavender and move on to some far more delicious vegetation to munch on. In the fourteen years we have been here on the farm and with all the hundreds of people we have talked to, there have been few stories of animals or insects making a meal out of lavender. I have heard of deer eating into the lavender, and in that case, I would be sure to keep them out with a perimeter.

There is the rare occasion that you could get aphids or, possibly, tiny worms in the spring. I have seen this only once in a small area of one of our fields. It is pretty rare and more of a nuisance than the cause of any real damage. You can spray your lavender plant with insecticidal soap, which is organic, so you will not be putting any chemicals into your plant.

There are only a few diseases that can attack your lavender: (1) types of root rot, (2) mosaic virus, and (3) dieback. Although dieback is not technically a disease, it can affect your plant. It is unlikely you will ever see any of these, and with some prevention techniques, you can avoid these from happening.

Root rot occurs when there is too much water in the soil and the roots contract a virus. Be sure to allow your plants to almost dry out before watering again. Overwatering allows the virus to get into the roots. It is the most common error in growing lavender and will kill your plant. This occurs quickly, and you cannot stop it. The plant will die quickly and look like dried brown sticks, no mistaking it. The best thing you can do is to remove the plant and not plant in that area again. You can also buy antifungal spray at the nursery and spray the area after removing the plant. Just know it is not organic, and you will have to continue treatment. Don't get too worried about this; it is rare, and you probably will never encounter this problem.

The exception with watering is that when your lavender is first planted, it will need more water to acclimate to its new environment. Too little water will allow the roots to dry and die, and too much water drowns them. If either of these happen and the plant begins to die, you will not be able to stop it.

Mosaic virus comes from smokers touching your plants. If you are a smoker, it is best to always sanitize your hands and wear gloves when working with or touching your plants. You can tell whether your lavender has this virus by the yellowing of the leaves. They take on the appearance of yellow blotching and look like they have a mosaic design on the leaf. If this happens, you cannot heal the plant.

Once you have determined this is occurring in your plant, you will need to remove the plant from your garden. Mosaic virus is contagious and will spread to your other plants and eventually kill them, so remove the sick plant immediately before it has time to spread and infect other plants. Do not put the affected plant in your compost pile or set it alongside the garden to take out later; dispose of it in the trash right away. This virus is airborne and can transfer to your other plants, so once you have accurately verified that the problem is truly mosaic virus, remove the plant immediately. Some have suggested burning the plant, but I do not recommend you do that. Just don't leave it lying around; trash it, and do not dispose of it in your compost pile.

Sometimes you will see some yellowing of the leaves; this can be due to too much water or moisture around the plant, so don't diagnose mosaic virus too soon. You can take a cutting to your nursery, and they should be able to identify it. Mosaic virus is not specific to lavender; it can affect your other plants as well.

Dieback seems to be showing up in lavender gardens more and more. Although this is not a virus, it nonetheless affects the plant. This happens when a portion of the lavender plant dies off. It is usually in the center or on the south-facing side of the plant and generally happens when you live in an area in which plants go dormant in the winter; it usually happens to the plants in the spring when temperatures fluctuate forty-plus degrees on any given day. This can cause dieback. It is not a disease per se but an occurrence. If you have the patience to wait about a year, it is possible the plant can repair itself. Cut out the dead part so the sun can get into the plant and then wait and wait and wait. It will come back.

Mulching

There's not much to say on this subject. Just *don't* do it. Mulching helps our gardens to hold in water for the roots of the plants. This is something that is not beneficial for lavender. Remember that lavender wants to be drenched and drained. Mulching will not allow this process to happen and will keep too much water in the soil and damage your plant.

This is pretty much all you need to know to have a beautifully growing lavender garden that will give you joy for years to come. So have fun, enjoy, and let me know how your garden grows.

You can contact the farm at info@purpleadobelavenderfarm.com.

Planting Your Lavender Checklist

⟶

Now you are ready to plant your garden. Below is a checklist so you can see whether you have done all the steps prior to planting. Then you are ready to plant.

1. You have selected an area in which your garden will be planted. ____
2. You have completed your garden design. ____
3. You have checked your soil for composition and drain ability. ____
4. You have chosen sun-loving plants, and the neighboring plants are comparable. ____
5. You have dug all of your holes and can see your design layout. ____
6. You have placed a shovelful of composted soil next to the hole and put one handful of Yum Yum Mix along with it. ____
7. You have installed your irrigation hoses so you can turn them on as soon as planting is completed. ____

Planting Instructions

⁓

WHEN YOU HAVE SELECTED WHERE your garden will be, it is time to choose your varieties. You have checked your soil for composition (no clay) and drain ability, assessed how much sun the area will get, and selected neighboring plants that are compatible. When your design is complete and drawn out, you are ready to begin planting.

Planting is the fun part. There are just a few important rules to follow to keep your plants strong and healthy.

1. Dig your holes, and lay a shovelful of compost and one handful of Yum Yum Mix next to each hole.
2. Place all plants (in their pots) inside the holes. Do not remove the plants from their pots prior to placing them in the ground, because it will give too much air to the roots.
3. Plant your lavender.

If you look at your plant, you will see a small trunk. It is important to plant it with that trunk above the soil level. It is like a tree—you would not plant the trunk of a tree below the soil level, and so it is with lavender.

Before placing your plant in the ground, open the roots just a little to encourage them to spread out and take hold. Not too much but enough to separate the compacted roots and dirt from how they were growing in the pot.

Place the plant in the hole, mixing half soil and half compost along with the entire amount of Yum Yum Mix.

Be sure that the plant level is placed in the hole exactly the same as it was when it was in the pot. Plant with no wells and no mounds, and remember—*no* mulching!

Plant in the morning or late afternoon. It is generally too hot to plant in midday, as the heat and sun of the day can be too stressful on the new plants.

You can place your irrigation hoses before or after the planting, but the plants must be watered as soon as the planting is complete. If you intend to plant over more than one day, the plants you have put in the ground will need to be watered right after the planting. Be sure to water thoroughly, and remember to drench and drain. They love this method of watering.

If, after planting, you see the heads of your lavender bend over and droop, know that this is how lavender deals with the stress and heat of the day. By the end of the day, they will pick back up. It does not mean they need water. People often make the mistake of giving them too much water and end up killing the plant.

One exception: if your plants are new, check the soil to see whether they actually do need water. If it is wet, then do not give them any additional water. When plants are new, it can be a bit tricky to figure out exactly when to water, and overwatering at this stage can be detrimental for your lavender. It will take up to a few weeks for your plants to get acclimated to their new environment. Be patient, and one day you will see that they have settled into their new home. You are on your way to enjoying one of your most beautiful gardens.

Dos and Don'ts of Growing Lavender

KEEP YOUR PLANTS HEALTHY AND alive by using these simple rules for growing lavender.

1. Plant your lavender in full sun.
2. Be sure to pick an area in which you have good drainage. If the soil does not drain well, it will eventually kill your lavender.
3. Do not plant in clay soil.
4. Do not plant on a mound, and do not make a well around your plant.
5. Plants should be irrigated from drippers—no overhead watering.
6. Lavender should be put on its own watering zone unless the other plants have the same watering needs and are of like-kind.
7. Don't forget to prune your lavender properly after the first year.
8. Do not mulch your lavender in the winter.
9. Do not transplant your lavender.
10. Do not allow smokers to work on or touch your plants; they could give the plants a virus.

You will have many years of enjoyment from your lavender if you follow these ten simple rules for growing lavender. You can expect to lose about 1 to 5 percent of your lavender per year; this is the nature of the plant. If your plants are happy where they're planted and have been planted properly, they will give you ten to fifteen years of beautiful flowers and immense joy as an added bonus.

PART 2

Caring for and Preserving Your Lavender, Harvest to Craft

‑⸱

It gives me great joy to offer you knowledge, essence, and beauty on the subject of growing lavender. For the purpose of this section, we will be dealing with two specific genera of lavender, *Lavendula angustifolia* and *Lavendula x intermedia*, simply put, English and French lavender. The quest for understanding lavender and how to grow and work with this amazing plant has never been so requested. Here in part 2 of this book, you will find a written account of simple, uncomplicated instructions on what to do with your lavender after it blooms.

Maintenance

Caring for your lavender is very easy and takes almost no maintenance. A couple of cuts here, a snip there, add some water, and voilà, you have beautiful lavender. It really can be that simple. If you follow the instructions in this book, you are off to a great start. Here in part 2 we will talk about how to maintain, harvest, prune, and preserve your lavender until you are ready to use it.

Lavender does not need a lot of attention, but it does have specific needs. It has been said to be one of the most loved plants of the twenty-first century. Its popularity has grown and is evidenced by the three hundred-plus lavender farms growing here in the US that span coast to coast and produce an abundance of lavender and lavender products.

The lavender plant is one of the easiest plants to grow. Depending on where you live, this will determine how much time you will put into caring for your lavender. If you live in a zone six or above, it is likely that your plants will have more than one blooming and will require a little more cutting to maintain your garden. For the purpose of this book, I will be discussing a midrange zone of four and five. If you live in a higher zone like six, seven, or eight, all the principals apply, but your plants will need to be cut again for your additional blooming season.

Lavender needs very little maintenance; it requires little water and no fertilizers or herbicides. Simply put, it is one of the easiest plants to grow and can offer amazing beauty and a deep feeling of peace.

Growing lavender is an easy process; weeding your garden will be the most work you will have to do with your lavender. Watering, harvesting, and pruning are just about all you will be doing. Lavender basically has no diseases or bugs that are interested in bothering your plants, and that is good news for you. It will make growing lavender not only desirable but also a pretty simple undertaking. You can have a beautiful garden with little to no maintenance.

Basically, you will plant, water, harvest, prune, and then repeat the process next year, except for the planting part. Lavender is a perennial plant and will give many years of growth and beauty.

HARVESTING

It is important that you harvest and prune your lavender plants yearly and do not allow the lavender to stay on the plant. Good housekeeping for your plant keeps it healthy and maintains the traditional dome shape. Otherwise, without the performance of these steps, it becomes long and leggy and basically unattractive.

Harvesting is a bit different than pruning. They are similar in that both require the cutting of the plant, but harvesting is the removing of the flowers along with the stems, and pruning is the cutting back of the plant. Both are a part of caring for its health and retaining the traditional dome shape of the lavender plant but are different processes. If you have ever seen a beautiful field of lavender in Provence, you will notice that they have dome shapes, creating the most stunning symmetrical forms. Harvesting keeps your plant healthy and will give you the most beautiful lavender bundles to make a craft with or to adorn your table with a vase of stunning lavender flowers. Pruning your plants is done after the lavender stems have been harvested.

Harvesting is done at different times. It really depends on what you want to do with your lavender. If you just want to leave the lavender in your garden to enjoy the beauty, then you can actually leave them uncut until the blooms have faded and lost their color. You will still be able to use your lavender for crafting, so don't cut it and throw it away; it will still have plenty of scent within it.

If you want to use your blooms for a bouquet, you will cut your stems back when the corolla blooms are open about 40 to 50 percent of their blooming. The corolla is the small tubular flower that comes out of the end of the lavender bud. Leaving the stems on the plant longer will allow the corolla to die and leave holes in the buds. This is not very attractive if you are using the stems for display.

To harvest your plant, you will need a good pair of hand pruners. They can be purchased at your local hardware or nursery store. Corona makes a fine pair of cutters, and if cared for, they will last you for many years to come.

To begin your harvesting, you will need the following items: a good pair of cutters, isopropyl alcohol in a spray bottle, and size three rubber bands. The alcohol is sprayed on your cutters before and after you finish cutting each plant. This is done to prevent the spreading of any disease from one plant to another. This is a good practice anywhere in your gardens. It will not harm the plant; it will sterilize your cutters.

Now you are ready to harvest those fragrant, lovely, divine flowers. You will begin by spraying alcohol onto your cutters to disinfect them. Then reach into your plant and take a handful of flowers in one hand while cutting with the other. Cut your flowers at the base of the stem. Do not cut into the plant itself, only cut to the base of the stem where it meets the plant. You can take ahold of a handful of flowers, probably twenty-five or thirty at a time for each cutting that will be added to your finished bundle. Once you have done this about three times, you will have enough stems to make the perfect bundle. Place them together in a bouquet. You should have between seventy-five and one hundred stems for each bundle. This is just the right size after drying to make a lovely bouquet for a table or for a crafting idea you may have.

To determine how many flowers to put into a bundle, you can measure by putting the tip of your thumb to the tip of your middle finger. This will give you a good measure of the size your bundle should be. There should be about seventy-five to one hundred stems. You do not want more than that amount in a bundle, as they can hold too much moisture while in the drying process and could mildew. If this happens, the bundle will no longer be good, and you will need to toss it out.

After you have cut the number of flowers you need to make your bundle, take your rubber band and wrap it around the bundle three times. The rubber band should rest about three inches from the bottom of the stem.

When you have completed your harvest, you can use the fresh bundles in a vase, or you could choose to dry them and use at a later date.

FRESH CUT

If you want to use your lavender in a fresh bouquet, this is pretty easy to do. There are just a couple of things you need to know about fresh-cut lavender. After you harvest your bundle, put it in water immediately. Snip a small amount off of the bottom of the stems so the stems will be fresh and open to take in some water. Contrary to popular belief, fresh lavender only needs a very small amount of water. It only takes in sips of water at a time. Add about one inch of water in the bottom of your vase. Using more could result in blackening of the stems, and then you will not be able to dry them for later use. No matter how tempted you are, only put a little bit of water in the bottom of the vase. You can change this water every other day to keep it fresh until they start to dry out. At this point, you can begin with the drying process to preserve your lavender or empty the water from the vase and allow them to air-dry right in the vase.

Drying

Now that you have decided to dry your lavender, this is how it is done. You can use large paper clips or a string and attach it to the rubber band that you put on the bundle. You will use this as a hanger. If you are using a string, just tie it to the rubber band so you can hang it from a hook. If you are using a paper clip, open up the end of the paper clip and insert that part under the rubber band you have around your bundle. Thread it by turning the paper clip over a few times so the rubber band ends up on the inside of the center of the clip. This creates a natural hanger for hanging purposes. At this point, your bundle is ready to hang to dry.

Deciding where to hang your lavender depends on how much space you have. If you have a few bundles, you can hang them in your closet and allow the lavender to drift into your clothing. If you have many plants, thus yielding a larger amount, you may want to consider hanging them in your garage or any dark room that will accommodate your harvest size.

If you hang them in a closet, you can put them on a hanger. Just be sure they have air space all around them for a perfect drying environment.

If you hang them in your garage, use a chain, which you can hang on a hook, and then put the paper clip in the openings of the chain, or on a wire or a string stretched out like a clothesline.

Hanging your flowers in a dark room will allow the lavender to retain its beautiful color and dry out properly. If they are dried in a bright room, they will fade. Depending on whether you live in a humid or dry climate, it will take between one and two weeks to dry. Be sure you are happy with where you hang them, as it is important to allow your bundles to completely dry out.

There are several ways to hang your lavender; you may find a way that suits your space better. Just be sure the bundles have airflow all around them so they dry perfectly. No matter how you choose to do this process, the lavender will fill any room with amazing scents.

PRESERVING

Now that you have finished harvesting, are you wondering, "What's next, what do I do with all the lavender?"

There is so much you can do with your lavender, but first, protecting it from the air, light, and dust by boxing it is important. This will preserve the bundles so they will be ready for later use.

Your bundles are now ready to preserve. This next step will not only protect them for later use, it will be economical and easy to store on a shelf in your garage. Lavender will retain its scent and stay fragrant well into the next year. You can preserve your lavender until you are ready to use it. That is the beauty of lavender: there is no waste to this plant—you can use every bit of it and use it whenever you want.

Preserving lavender is a simple process and requires little time. You will need a box or boxes depending on how many bundles you have and tissue paper to cover each layer.

You will start by putting a layer of tissue paper to cover the bottom of the box, then begin laying your bundles in the box. You can fill the entire bottom of the box before you begin your next layer, making sure to cover the lavender entirely. Do not push down or cram in more bundles than fit comfortably in the first layer, as you may break the stems. Continue layering tissue and bundles until you have reached the top of the box. Seal it with tape, label it with the date, and voilà, you have safely saved your lavender to be used at your convenience and need at a later date. That is all there is to it. It is simple, easy, and compact. Using tissue and boxes allows the lavender to breathe, which is important in the preservation step. Totes will hold in the scent, but if there is heat in the area you store them, this could cause the buds to fall off the stem. It is better to use a cardboard box.

Pruning Your Lavender

Pruning your lavender plant is probably one of the most important factors in growing a healthy, beautiful plant. Because lavender is a perennial, it should be trimmed every year. Pruning keeps the traditional dome shape of the plant. Usually it is not necessary to prune the first year, especially if your plant is small, but if you purchase a larger size, it will need trimming. Traditionally, trimming back your plant is done the second season after blooming. This keeps the plant full and looking beautiful. If this is not done, your plant will become leggy with long, hard wood branches, and tufts of lavender will grow at the end of the branches. Once this happens, it is not possible to return it to its original and traditional dome shape.

When to prune is always a question. Should you prune in the spring or in the fall? I prefer to prune our plants in the fall no later than October. Of course, this depends on where you live. If you live in a higher zone, such as seven or eight, you could still be in blooming season. So be sure to wait until your blooming season has finished for the year.

Here in New Mexico, our blooming season ends by August, and we prune just after we harvest. The farm has five thousand plants, so it makes sense for us to harvest and prune all at the same time so we do not need to revisit the fields for a second time. In your garden, it could be a different story. You could harvest your plants and come back a month later and prune.

This is not a difficult or time-consuming process. Pruning is an easy process and literally takes just minutes on each plant. Pruning your plant will keep your plant healthy and looking lovely year after year. The process can be done in a couple of ways. If you want to spend time with your plants, you can prune by hand using garden cutters. If you are in a hurry and just want to get the task done, you can actually use pruners that are battery operated or even electric. You could prune your plant in less than a minute using a battery or electric hand trimmer. These can be purchase relatively inexpensively at your local hardware store. They require no oil or gas, which is a good thing for your plant. You don't want to use anything that would leave a residue on your lavender plant.

Either of these methods are fine; it is your preference. Cutting back your lavender is really no different than cutting back any perennials in your garden. The purpose is to keep them full, healthy, and thriving year after year.

Pruning will force life back into the plant, and it will grow more lateral stems that will fill in the growth and create a robust and full plant. The process of pruning is done once a year, and that is all the trimming your plant will need.

In determining how much to trim back, this will depend on how much growth the plant has had during the year. A good rule of thumb is to cut it back one-third of its *new* growth. Once you have cut off the flowers, you will be able to see how much new growth has occurred during the season. Look closely, and you will be able to see new growth. It is usually no more than a couple of inches. Be sure you are looking at the new growth. New growth is the green bushy part of the plant—it is not the entire plant. Just start snipping back, cutting evenly on the plant, and trim into a dome shape.

To watch a video on pruning lavender, go to our website and download a quick lesson on how to prune your lavender: www.purpleadobelavenderfarm.com.

Once you have completed this step, there is literally nothing else you need to do until the new growing season begins except some watering.

Winter Watering
Even after you harvest and prune your lavender, it still needs water. You will cut back on the amount of water in a couple of stages. Before winter starts, zones four and five will water maybe every ten days to two weeks, depending on how much rain you have gotten. If there is a lot of rain in your area, you will not need to water, but if it is hot and dry, then every ten days should do it. If you are in zones six, seven, or eight, you may need to water once a week, and again, this will depend on whether you get a lot of rain. If you do, you will not need to water. Remember, lavender is an arid plant and prefers less rather than more water. During winter months, your plants still need water. You will only water once a month until they begin to come into growing season in the spring. When spring comes around, you will water thoroughly after any danger of the last frost has passed. This will signal the plant to wake up and start its new season.

PART 3
Crafting with Lavender

—◦—

WHAT WILL YOU DO WITH your lavender now that you have successfully harvested, pruned, and packed it away safely? You will have plenty of time to decide how you will use it.

There are many choices available to you when deciding what you are going to use your lavender for and when you are going to need it. You may want to save it until the holidays and make personalized holiday gifts, or if you have a special birthday coming, you can save it until you are ready to use it. It is a lovely, unique gift that came from your garden—what could be better.

Here are a few ideas. Have a lavender dinner party and place beautiful vases of aromatic fresh-cut lavender all through your home. Fill a beautiful decorative bowl of lavender heads (just cut them from the stems) in the guest bathroom and add a couple of rose heads or petals to create a lovely display and amazing natural scents for your guests to enjoy. Use some English lavender buds in a dessert, or serve a special lavender cocktail. Use your culinary imagination for endless dishes, and delight your friends with lavender from your garden to your table. Show it off to all your friends, and create an amazing culinary experience.

Take time and design your own aromatic lavender sachets, eye pillow, or neck pillow for gift giving. Search antique shops looking for antique linen napkins for a more formal look to your sachets. Think about using the fabric from an old, worn-out tablecloth, T-shirt, or blouse ready to be tossed. Instead of throwing it away, recycle it into a lovely sachet for your drawers or to put under your pillow to help you sleep at night. Use any fabric you may have on hand to design a unique look and give as a gift. Search the fabric stores or secondhand stores to find unusual fabrics.

You can be creative in making a lavender bundle with dozens of ways to adorn them by adding fresh flowers from your garden or the market. Whether the lavender is stand-alone in a vase or there to highlight a bouquet, it will not disappoint.

If it is culinary lavender, which is typically English, you can use it in many of your cooking dishes; the ideas are literally endless. If you want to cook with lavender and do not know how, there are many lavender cookbooks available to choose from. We have a lovely comprehensive cookbook on our website that comes with a packet of culinary lavender. Or try experimenting on your own. Just remember it is an herb and a little goes a long way. Cook with the mind-set that less is more. Lavender is strong when used as an herb—do not over-season.

There are so many uses for lavender; this could be a book all by itself. You can make tinctures, potions and balms and scrubs and bath bombs, and of course things to adorn your home. All you have to do is use your imagination; the ideas are endless.

Now that you have preserved your lavender, you will be able to use it throughout the year until your next harvest comes. If you have packed it properly, it will preserve beautifully. You can make lovely items for your own home or make a special gift for friends. Everyone loves lavender and will appreciate your special creative gift; home-made lavender gifts are something that cannot be bought in stores.

Any way you use it, you will enjoy your homegrown lavender. Drying your lavender will afford you multiple options for using your lavender in your own time when it is convenient for you. Lavender will keep its scent for years, so there is no urgency to use it immediately.

CLEANING YOUR LAVENDER BUDS

If you are working on a project that requires lavender buds rather than a bundle, you will have to clean it first. Here's how: lay out a 20 x 20 sheet of paper or a bag that the buds will fall into; any will work. Take your bundle between your hands, and move your hands back and forth over the buds of the bundle so they start to fall off the stems. Continue to do this until all the buds are free from the stems and until you have the desired amount of buds on your paper. Pick out any stems that may have fallen with your buds.

Now use a wire colander to sift the lavender dust from the buds. All lavender has lavender dust. The buds will be cleaner and less of an allergen if you remove the dust. Put your buds in a wire-screened colander, and begin sifting the dust onto a large sheet of paper or into a trash receptacle. You will not want to save the dust. There, that is all there is to it. You can use your buds directly or put them in a ziplock bag and seal it. This will retain the scent of the lavender and keep it fresh until you are ready to use it.

Some of the following formulas call for lavender essential oil in addition to the botanical. This is optional, and you can just use the fresh or dried botanical lavender buds or bundles. Lavender essential oil can be purchased online, in a health food store, or on our website at www.purpleadobelavenderfarm.com. Be sure when purchasing lavender essential oil it is called essential oil and not fragrance or parfum. Essential oil is the true distillation from the flower itself, and fragrance or parfum is chemically produced. That goes for any oils or bath and body products you purchase. You can be sure you are getting essential oil if you read the label and look for this distinction in the ingredients.

If you are ready to try your hand at some fun and creative ideas using your lavender, let's get to it. Most of your needs can either be purchased at the grocery store or online. Any containers you need can be purchased online, at a hobby store, or at a health food store. Here are some ideas for you to experiment with:

Bath and Body

- lip balm
- bath salts
- dryer bags

Scented Room

- room and linen spray
- potpourri
- sachets and travel sachets

Culinary

- lavender syrup
- summer lavender raspberry spritzer
- favorite teas
- lavender sugar

Bath and Body

Lavender Lip Balm

It is always special to carry a little lavender lip balm in your pocket or purse to soothe dry lips. Here is an easy lip balm recipe you can make at home in your kitchen.

You will need:
small lip balm tins, tubes, or a small jar
glass measuring cup
stirring utensil
microwave-safe cling wrap
candy thermometer

Ingredients:
8 ounces olive oil
1 ounce beeswax or soy wax pearls or cubes
1½ teaspoon lavender essential oil (you will have to buy this; it is not made from your buds)

Instructions:
Cover measuring cup with cling wrap and poke four holes in the wrap to vent. Melt the wax along with the olive oil slowly in the glass measuring cup in a microwave. Begin melting for thirty seconds, then

continue in fifteen-second increments and stir in between until the pearls have melted. You can also use a double boiler on top of the stove to melt ingredients. When all is melted, check temperature. When temperature reaches 150°F, add essential oil. Stir well and pour into containers. Allow to cool and become opaque before closing lids. Enjoy.

Bath Salts

Bath salts are healing to the body. Salt hydrates and soothes tired, aching muscles. Add lavender to it, and it is a wonderful spa treatment in your own home. Lavender is known for its calming ability. Try this easy-to-make formula, and relax into a hot tub infused with lavender bath salts. This will quiet and rejuvenate your body, mind, and spirit.

You will need:
measuring cup
mixing bowl
spoon
jar for storage

Ingredients:
1 cup salts (Mediterranean, Dead Sea, or Himalayan salt)
½ cup Epsom salt
20 drops lavender essential oil
2 tablespoons lavender buds (if you do not want the buds floating in the bath, use a sachet bag to put your buds in; optional)

Instructions:
Mix salt and Epsom salt together in a bowl. Once the salts are mixed thoroughly, add your buds and combine. You can now add your essential oil; mix thoroughly. Save in a jar for later use, or add directly to your bath. You only need four ounces for a therapeutic bath, but if you really want a spa experience, just add all the salt at once into your bath and enjoy. Ahhhh.

DRYER BAGS

You can toss these bags into your dryer to add a lavender scent to your sheets, towels, or any garment you like. You will need large sealable tea bags to make these. You can purchase these at your local hobby store or online. Amazon carries them as well. You will fill these and use an iron to seal the edge. The finished lavender bag can be used several times. Just give it a crush before you toss it into the dryer to release the essential oil from the buds. It is best to toss it in the dryer after about ten minutes when a good bit of moisture has been removed from the laundry. Stack four bags and tie with a decorative ribbon and a bow. They are perfect for gift giving.

You will need:
large sealable tea bags
clothes iron
tablespoon

Ingredients:
3–4 tablespoons cleaned lavender buds

Instructions:
Put the lavender buds into the tea bag. Settle all the lavender in the bottom of the bag, then iron the open edge with the warm iron to seal the edge. That's it! Give the bag a crush to release the essential oil scent from the buds, and toss it into your dryer.

Scented Room

Room and Linen Spray

Keep your room as fresh as a lavender field. This is so easy to make you will never be without it. Use this easy formula to sweeten the scent of your sheets and spray lavender in your room. Lavender does not stain and will leave nothing but a sweet scent of lavender flowers wherever you use it. You will need to use lavender essential oil for this recipe.

You will need:
one 8-ounce bottle with sprayer
tablespoon
funnel
measuring cup

Ingredients:
6 ounces distilled water (spring water is fine too)
3 tablespoons vodka (optional)
10 drops lavender essential oil

Instructions:
Fill measuring cup with six ounces of water, then add three table-spoons of vodka (optional if you do not want the smell of alcohol).

Then add ten drops of lavender essential oil. You can add more essential oil if you like a stronger scent. Mix well and fill your bottle using the funnel. Shake and spray your room generously. You can spray this on your sheets and clothing. Remember, lavender does not stain, so do not hesitate to spray it on liberally. Optional: you can add other essential oils to your homemade sprays to complement the lavender scent.

LAVENDER AND ROSE POTPOURRI

Have you ever noticed all the surprises in your garden when spring comes around? There are new flowers perfect for drying or using fresh and adding to your lavender potpourri as a complement. If you do not have flowers in your garden, there are dozens of choices at your grocery store. Pick them by color, scent, or size to complement your lavender potpourri. They can be used fresh or dried. Snip the flower heads off, and allow them to dry in the bowl if you like. Lavender buds will be the base of your potpourri; everything else will be the complement and accent to enhance the visual bowl of lovely flowers.

You will need:
mixing bowl
spoon
cutters for snipping flowers

Ingredients:
1–2 cups lavender buds.
1 cup fresh flower heads (of choice)
5 drops lavender essential oil (optional)
dried rose petals
dried rose hips
dried herbs from your garden (anything that looks pretty)

Instructions:
Mix all your ingredients together and place in a decorative bowl and place around your home or in the guest bathroom to add a lovely scent for your guests to enjoy. Adding roses or any other dried flowers to the bowl will enhance the beauty of your potpourri. Optional: you can add a few drops of lavender essential oil to the flowers in the bowl. Some folks like the additional scent of the lavender essential oil, and others prefer the scent of the herbal lavender botanical alone.

LACE HANKIE SACHETS
You will need:
lace hankie (visit a vintage shop and look for a lady's hankie with lace edging)
rubber band
ribbon for decoration

Ingredients:
¼ cup flax seed (this keeps your sachets from turning crunchy)
½ cup lavender buds
Lavender essential oil (optional)

Instructions:
Lay your hankie flat, and fill the center with about one-half cup of ingredients. Optional: add a few drops of lavender oil to the buds. Although the oil is not necessary, some crafters enjoy adding a few drops of essential oil. Dried lavender alone has an amazing scent, and will last for years, so you do not need to use the oil if you choose not to. Scoop up the hankie, and bring all sides together, making a ball with the ingredients. Put a rubber band around it a few times to secure it. Add your favorite ribbon over the rubber band to finish your sachet. Use in your drawers or hang in your closet to add a lavender scent. Hang on your guest bathroom door with a tag that says, "Squeeze me." This will release the essential oil inside your sachet.

Travel Sachets

Travel sachets are pretty much the same as the lace hankie sachets, with a couple of adjustments. When you travel, you will want your sachet to be a bit more functional than decorative. You will not need flax seed for this. You want the full strength of the lavender. When traveling, I like my room smelling fresh, and we all know that is not always the case. Use the lavender travel sachets to freshen and leave your room with scents of a lavender field. Remember, always give them a good crush before using them to release the essential oil. Place them everywhere in the hotel room—under pillows, in drawers, on cabinets—to keep your room smelling lavender fresh.

You will need:
1 package 2 x 3 or 3 x 4 sewn sachet bags (you can find these online or at Michaels)
1 gallon-size ziplock bag
teaspoon

Ingredients:
4 cups lavender buds (approx.)
lavender essential oil (optional)

Instructions:
Fill each bag using your teaspoon to the desired fullness. Tie off, and that's it! Pretty simple, isn't it? Store them in your ziplock bag, and carry it with you when you travel. This will keep your sachets fresh and ready for use when you are on the road.

Culinary Recipes

 ~~⌐

Ways to Use Your Culinary Lavender

Ground—In most of your recipes, you will want to grind your lavender. Keep a mason jar filled with crushed lavender in your spice cabinet so it is ready to use. Grinding lavender is done best in a grinder of its own. We use a coffee grinder. This gives you the perfect consistency for seasoning. Ground lavender should look like ground sage. It is light and fluffy.

Whole Bud—Using the whole bud is mostly for decorating your baking. It is quite impressive with a few beautiful buds on top of your ice cream, cookies, or cake. However, for the most part, your lavender seasoning should come from ground buds. It is not particularly tasty to find a whole lavender bud in your culinary dishes.

Sprigs—Whether you use dried lavender or a fresh sprig, it can be quite lovely adorning your finished culinary creation. Sprigs are used as a decoration rather than for being eaten.

Fresh lavender can be used if your dish is being eaten the same day you make it, but do not use fresh lavender in dishes that will be saved or held in reserve in a recipe such as pastry, beverages, or uncooked dishes. It could mildew or turn bad and create bacteria in your recipe because of the moisture in the flower. As long as you use flowers that have been dried, you can save it in your recipe with no worry. It is then considered an herb and is safe for storage.

There are so many recipes you can make using culinary lavender. You will want to use English lavender from your garden for your culinary dishes. Here are a few that will take you a long way and inspire your imagination.

Lavender Syrup

You can use lavender syrup by adding it to any of your wet recipes. Lavender syrup is one of the basics in your lavender cupboard. It is a staple in the lavender culinary world. It is good to have some on hand when a recipe calls for it.

Your syrup can be used in the desired amount (to taste) in lemonade, iced or hot tea. It is yummy in a cappuccino or latte. Add syrup to a specialty cocktail to sweeten and give a lovely lavender flavor to your creation. This will amaze your friends at your lavender-themed dinner party. Try making your summer spritzers at a lady's lavender luncheon.

You will need:
2-quart saucepan
measuring cup
spoon
fine metal sieve
2-quart bottles or mason jars
label

Ingredients:
2 cups cane sugar
8 cups water
½ cup culinary lavender (dried)
¼ teaspoon lemon juice

Instructions:
Boil four cups of the water. Add sugar to boiling water; reduce and simmer on a gentle rolling boil until all sugar is completely dissolved. Remove pan from heat; add lavender and stir. Allow lavender to steep

in sugar water for two hours. Fill pot with reserved four cups of water, and add the lemon juice to your lavender syrup to give it a bit of color. Strain your syrup through a fine sieve strainer into another bowl to remove all the buds. Pour into bottle or mason jar using a funnel, and put a label with the date on it. Store in your refrigerator for up to one month. Add desired amount to any beverage to suit your own taste. This is a quick and easy way to have lavender essence on hand to add to your culinary creations. Makes two quarts.

Summer Lavender Raspberry Spritzer

6 ounces mineral water
1-ounce raspberry syrup
1–2 tablespoons lavender syrup (to taste)
3 fresh raspberries
1 sprig fresh spearmint
ice cubes

Instructions:
Fill a glass half full with ice. Pour raspberry syrup over ice. Add mineral water. Top with lavender syrup. Crush spearmint between your fingers to release the oil and place in the glass. Top with raspberries, a sprig of lavender, and a pink straw. This is so refreshing on a hot summer day. You will love it. Makes one eight-ounce serving.

FAVORITE TEAS

This is the easiest way to make an amazing tea. You will need culinary lavender from your garden. Remember to use only English lavender; do not use French lavenders, as they are quite strong with camphor. This can ruin a perfectly wonderful flavor and the experience of enjoying your favorite tea. You will need five to six little dried buds. Take a few of the buds, crush them between your fingers, and place them in a tea ball along with your favorite tea. Place the tea ball in a cup of hot water and allow to steep. Not only will you enjoy your favorite tea, now you can enjoy it with a hint of lavender from your garden.

LAVENDER SUGAR
You will need:
mixing bowl
measuring spoon
spoon
coffee grinder
glass or plastic container with lid

Ingredients:
1 cup cane sugar
1 tablespoon ground culinary lavender (dried)

Instructions:
Using your coffee grinder, grind one tablespoon of culinary buds. When ground, they should look light and fluffy. Mix the sugar and the ground lavender buds together, and place in a container; mix again and seal. It should take a few days for the lavender to completely infuse into the sugar. This is delicious on top of cakes, sugar cookies, try it on cinnamon toast, or use in recipes that call for sugar. Add a bit of lavender to your sweet culinary dishes.

Notes and Designs

Notes and Designs

Notes and Designs

Notes and Designs

Notes and Designs

Made in the USA
Middletown, DE
28 May 2022